Kristofer Coleman's *I Didn't Use to Be Like This* is a collection of poems set against the backdrop of an adulthood of mental illness, personal loss and disillusionment. The works speak to a very contemporary outlook on life with themes which are universally relevant and relatable. It is at times brutally honest, emotional and highly reflective, but never boring.

This book is dedicated to my mum and dad, Jane Coleman and Norman Coleman. You are my best friends.

Kristofer Coleman

I Didn't Use to Be Like This

AUSTIN MACAULEY PUBLISHERS®
LONDON · CAMBRIDGE · NEW YORK · SHARJAH

A CIP catalogue record for this title is available from the British Library.

ISBN 9781035850693 (Paperback)
ISBN 9781035850709 (ePub e-book)

www.austinmacauley.com

First Published 2024
Austin Macauley Publishers Ltd®
1 Canada Square
Canary Wharf
London
E14 5AA

Special thanks to Marilyn Reid for her faith, advice and encouragement. Without her, this book would not exist.

Also, credit for the sketches goes to Kristofer Coleman.

Inner (And Outer) Conflict

If, in peacetime, I despair,
Then in war, what hope is there?
There's no such thing as a winnable war.
Just the ones who lose, and those who lose more.

'Insert name here' for those who impose
This numbing misery that none of us chose.
Here's what I have, less than ever before,
And here's what you have, yet you want more.

For every atrocity, for each transgression,
We try to retaliate without aggression.
But where sits the line, and how long before
We become exactly what we abhor.

I pray that love and kindness prevail
In the face of universal betrayal.
Because which side is which, and who can we trust?
Before it's too late and our world turns to dust

Medication Time

Shapes dance across my eyes,
The beauty of maths.
Kaleidoscopic art,
From numerical paths
And patterns,
The visual representation
Of neurons firing.
A firm indication
My brain is rewiring.
Correcting malfunctions.
At least that's what I hope,
It's the sole purpose of the doctor's dope.

This is the product of a pill for good.
If I keep taking it, in time, I should,
Manage to repair the damage within,
And start to feel normal again.

Exit the shapes, from foreground to back.
Images take centre stage,
In tune with my thoughts, none of them good
And getting no better, I'll wage.
Existential angst,
The precursor for sleep,
Preventing transition from shallow to deep.
Electric shocks stab my brain,
Looking for slumber to spoil.
Will I exit this evening still sane?
As I burn the last of the midnight oil.

This is the product of a pill for good.
If I keep taking it, in time, I should,
Manage to repair the damage within,
And start to feel normal again.

Who Says the Icebergs
Are Melting?

Once you start, you can't refrain,
It induces despair you cannot contain.
They say it causes tiny holes in the brain
The consequences of cocaine.

Your face becomes a road map of pain
Optimism fades and motivation will wane.
Only the disciplined, or evil, will gain
Further prerequisites of cocaine.

More and more needed, for the high to maintain
The devil incarnate, polluting every vein.
Once it's finished, you may not be sane
That's the legacy of cocaine.

…and this is the tip of a giant, white iceberg.

A Brief Moment of Clarity

How have I survived all these years?
Mountains of pain, oceans of tears
I have walked the beautiful and the desolate
And all this time remained resolute
That redemption is just beyond where I am now
But it continues to evade me somehow
If I could've planted a flower when I did not yet know
Nature's incredible power, and the seeds how to sow
I may have realised what I now know, not so late
And I wouldn't feel like a middle-aged reprobate

My Statement

I feel that, particularly with the onset of the 21st century, we are witnessing nothing short of the complete collapse of civilised society. And it goes beyond the mere passive indifference to illegal foreign wars and seemingly faraway religious genocide, all in the face of the utmost domestic political corruption. We are entering a new phase where an absolute drainage of faith in humanity is leading to a profound mistrust in everything and everyone.

In this new vision of hell, we are beginning to accept, as reality, that mankind, without exception, is condemned to failure and death with a permanence never before experienced, and survival itself preempts existence.

I have stood on the precipice of reality and stared for a thousand miles. I saw nothing but darkness in every direction.

Nostalgia

That warm feeling you cannot pin down
It makes us simultaneously happy and sad
We hear songs we hated at the time
And recognise them as anthems from our youth
What is this emotion, so strong in beguile,
more powerful than love itself?
Like the dearest of hugs, we embrace it every time without fail.

Slaves to our feelings is what we are.
We crave the happiness we used to know,
But there is no going back.
Yet we cannot stop yearning for the past.
What futility in our reflections!
Our dreams recreate what we have lost,
But we will inevitably wake and lose it all over again.

How cruel our minds can be,
To make us relive the torture of what no longer is.
And in twenty years' time, I will yearn for the present.
The rose-tinted lens of retrospect will strike again;
Maybe, just maybe, I will appreciate what I have then.

Lime Green Jelly and Ice Cream

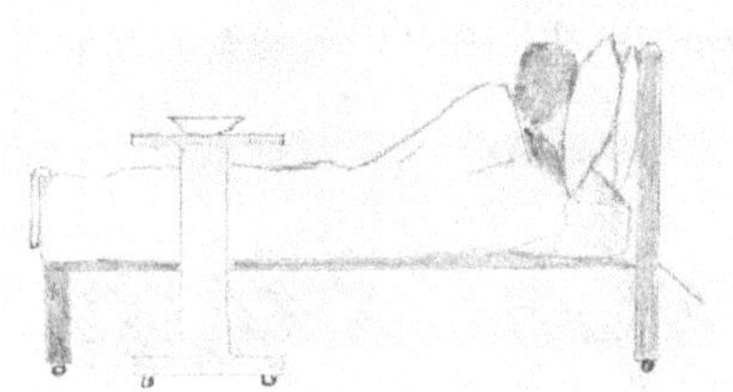

I had an operation back in '82, when I was three,
A cataract from my right eye was my fee.
My reward I was not to see
Was some ice cream and lime green jelly.

An unfair trade for my right eye, I now see,
For the surgeon mislaid, for that day, his ability
To perform his task proficiently,
And left me blind to a percentage of fifty.

After the op, I awoke
To see a pudding, most bespoke,
Just for me, lime green jelly and ice cream.
At age three, it was like a dream.

Never before had I seen such green,
With luminescent glow from inside with an outward sheen,
And a cuboid of gently melting ice cream,
Creating a sauce of marbled lime green.
It was the best thing I'd ever seen.

Yet, I could not rouse myself to dig deep,
For the anaesthetic forced me to sleep.
Perhaps if I shut my eyes for a little while,
It would still be there when I woke.
"Kris, don't be so infantile."

My bounty, when my eyes reopened, had turned to smoke.
Gone forever, and never to return,
Probably the first time my stomach was to cry and churn
At what could have been, my lost treasure of green.
The first of many wasted opportunities it would seem.

Night Time

A different world is what it is,
Stare at the stars and wonder.
Nature's blanket we all hide under
In isolation we seek.

Exposure strengthens the night's resolve,
We must embrace the cold and unseen thunder
For our worries to dissolve, our problems to be solved.
The moon's magical glow betrays what goes asunder.
So many demons in the night,
Their nocturnal subculture avoids the light.

The owls bear witness, their big eyes surveying,
Whilst we lie in our beds, quietly praying
That no harm shall come to us,
The one quiet passenger on a boisterous bus.

They say in the night time, the jungle comes alive,
Largely missed by those who are nine to five.
Its intrigue and menace goes seemingly unseen
By those who live and serve in between.

This is indeed 'the killing time,'
Whether in minutes or years,
A sudden horror, or decades of tears.
Pick your moment and disappear.

The Lone Swordsman

In 1992, a mix tape by you.
It had a preacher talking over some song or two.
I had no idea who you were,
And the indelible mark you had already made.
Still, I listened to references I could infer.
The Lone Swordsman was already sharpening his blade.

On account of my reduced age,
It was very difficult to get on the same page.
But gradually, as your productions were released,
My confusion and my doubt ceased.

Now every tune from that mix is ingrained,
And my mind and memory are forever stained
With the greatest possible scuffs and marks.
My neurons fired every time your imagination sparked.

We never met, and you probably could've lived till seventy,
And the same would be true.
But, my god, I wish I'd met you.

So many questions I would have, Mr Sabres,
Smokebelch II, Stockwell Steppas.
The reason I kept awake my neighbours,
When playing your music.
Which I still am, and you'll never know.
The curtains have not yet been drawn on Mr. Weatherall's show.

Hallucinogen

'I believe, with the advent of acid, we discovered a new way to think.' (Ken Kesey)

Acid leaks out every pore,
Acrid memories of what I've done before.
My short-term memory is no more,
The shop's open, but there's nothing in store.

Reality is no longer what it once was,
It's twisted and contorted, because
I took a substance many years ago,
Knowing not what I was to know.

If I had, I may have thought twice,
Back in the day, when I was still willing to throw the dice
And take a chance on uncertainty,
Assuming things would go my way.

They did not.

Absolute Beginners

We're six months in, I still don't know what you're thinking,
Except for that look of disapproval when I'm drinking.
We walk together, but you're not where I am,
I try speaking, but you don't give a damn.
You have your own agenda, which I hope includes me;
I wonder if the relationship I have craved will ever be.

Perhaps I am asking too much
To expect that our love is mutual, and I should be treated as such.
If only we could just talk and speak our minds,
You pull the lead, I trail behind.
I look forward to the day
When we both think the same way.

On the TV, we'll watch shite, on a Friday and Saturday night,
Share TV dinners, we'll be winners,
No longer absolute beginners.
I miss you, Susie.

Sitting In the Dark

For over twenty years, I have searched for the light,
Chopping through the foliage of darkness with no end in sight.
Darkness is solitude but also isolation,
Fifty shades of grey, determined by my motivation.

Some two decades plus, just when I start to prevail,
My ambitions are once again determined to fail.
What on Earth could be so cruel?
But the price of war and the price of fuel.

Those who are financially well-endowed
Line their pockets further and thicken the shroud
Of all that I have sought to escape these years,
But this time round, I am not alone in my fears.

Collectively, we are squeezed to within an inch of our existence,
Due to the legacy of greed and its guaranteed subsistence
On the misery of us, the ordinary folk,
Held in bondage of an inescapable choke.

It seems this winter, on which we are about to embark,
We will, all of us, be sitting in the dark.
(September 2022)

Omg

Our humanity seems to hang in the balance.
We are conditioned to accept the horrors we see on TV,
Like documentaries on the Holocaust, or slavery.
It makes us sick, what our predecessors have done.
How could they have thought it was okay?
And yet, it's still happening today.
People who have nothing, forced to accept even less,
While others bathe in a life of excess.
I ask, what kind of god would allow this to continue?
Certainly not one that I wish I ever knew.

Painted Smiles, Tainted Miles

Charity is a massive falsehood.
Do you do it because of the ads?
Trying to eat your food
When the child with the big eyes who can't see
Looks at the camera, and your stomach feels hollow.
But for £3 a month, you can ease their sorrows and set them free.

The geography of where we're born
Doesn't make us any less forlorn.
We try to feel their pain,
An exercise completely in vain.

If I could, I would make everything equal.
But like the original trilogy, there should be no sequel.
I watch 'Desperate Housewives' in utter despair.
Could there be a greater example of what is unfair?
People living in obscene and profound opulence and colossal ignorance.
Can they not see that there are so many in infinitely graver circumstances?

Keep The Masses
from Majority

Man on the TV says he understands,
But he just says what's right so he can wash his hands.
He takes money out my pocket and he lines his own,
Without any sense of shame or a need to atone.

The bills keep going up and the pay stays down,
All the shops are boarded up and there's no one in town.
Everybody's back is up and our nerves are exposed,
A single mother lost two stones 'cause the food bank closed.

Meanwhile, at the other end, the rich folks sit,
The rest of us are dying and they don't give a shit.
It's a grim situation, unlikely to change;
Equality, by day, grows further out of range.

I (Who Have Nothing)

I wish I could turn back the clock,
To the time when I had something.
But I have nothing,
The empty fishing boat sitting at the dock.

I am reminded at every turn
What could have been,
How many fingers to burn?
Over things I should have foreseen.

I will truly never be well-endowed
Financially, socially, physically or mentally.
If only I could discard this shroud,
Of never having achieved any kind of human quality.

I am broke,
I have nothing to offer, at all.
No fire to stoke,
No contribution to make, however small.

All I do is take,
And give nothing back.
I am neither genuine or fake,
Even I think I deserve a smack.

But nobody can hit me harder than I hit myself,
Quite literally, I punch myself awake every night,
In a vain attempt to stand and fight
The demons and horrors that torment me.
My own mind is my worst enemy.

I hope, if it's there, I will go to heaven,
Because I've already been to hell.

Growing Down

As we lament the ever-quickening passage of time, our hearts
ache evermore.
Less invincibility, more invisibility;
Seeking questions to the answers we already know.
Our expectations finally hit the floor.

My patience, like my hair, is gradually thinning,
They fade with my optimism.
And with each day that passes,
I'm closer to the end than the beginning.

Perhaps at this point there is nothing to lose,
On a daily basis, I question my own contribution.
Do I help others or just myself in this failing global institution?
Am I the bomb in all this, or simply the fuse?

My fist grasps desperately at the sands of faith,
Each loss I try to reverse in vain.
But perhaps in this loss, there can be gain,
So long as a few grains of faith remain.

Sleep

My best friend, and my worst enemy,
I bathe in your bliss,
Until I need a piss.
But my indolence serves me well,
No sleep is hell.
Do what you have to,
And re-embark into the unknown.
Eat and sleep, that's my comfort zone.
Too much gets you down,
Too little makes you frown.
At the very least,
Sleep is a complicated beast.

Systematic

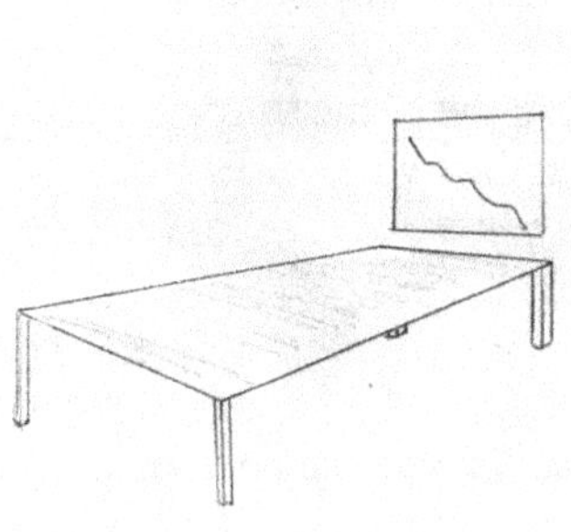

'All governments are liars and murderers' (Bill Hicks)

It's built into their DNA,
Fuck everyone else as long as you're OK.
'They' may suffer but you will proffer,
So long as you stick to the hymn sheet,
And you say nothing, they will never defeat you,
And all those who are like you,
Because it's that fucking easy.
Our government's disregard for us makes me queasy.

These are the people, if given the chance,
Slavery would still exist and would advance
To the point where we are all
Just trash beneath their feet,
And a force which is easy to defeat.

Inaction is the folly on which they rely,
We have our life, we work, then we die.
Too busy to take notice, we are forced to endure
A life that is polluted, and utterly impure.

The Merits of An Early Start

Cold, so cold on a winter morning,
Those who don't wake early, heed this warning.
The wind cuts through and aches your very bones,
Down to the marrow, invoking flu-like symptoms.
But there is something redemptive in this pain:
If you fight through, there is something to gain.
As you look up at the drawn curtains in envy of those who still
sleep,
You may, if you allow yourself, learn a lesson very deep.
For little in this world worth having comes without toil,
Whether you deliver the milk, or work the soil.
Being up early lets you see the best of the day;
If you can do at least that, you're on your way
To see the sweetest of life, and all it has to offer.
This is my experience and what I'd like to proffer.

The transition from night to day is something we should all
witness,
Feeding our souls and erasing the shit-ness
Which we are forced to endure on a daily basis.
We are all, without the morning, existing in stasis
– a purgatory of perpetual disappointment.
For the grazes of life, morning is ointment.
So enjoy the early hours, they carry much weight,
And may ease the passage to your uneasy fate.

Tomorrow Will Be a
Better Day

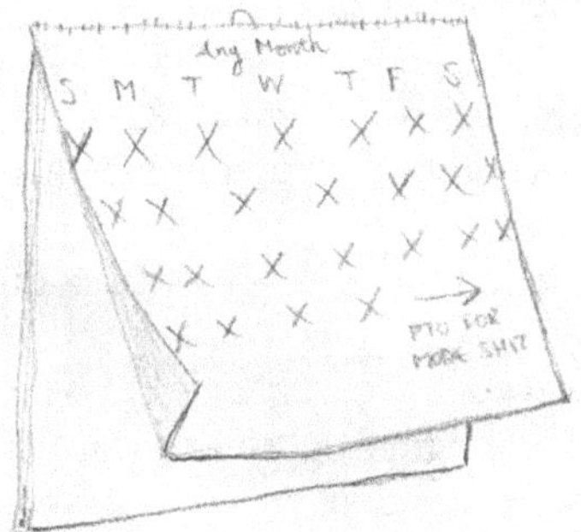

To myself, that's what I used to say
When events conspired to not go my way.
Someone I once knew dies every other day;
Faith is in short supply, all but drained away.
Leaving us in this collective depression, an omnipresent malaise,
I dare not have hope for future days.
To believe that tomorrow will be a better day
Is like pissing in the wind, I say.

I do believe in the power of human love,
But I just don't think any of it's coming from some divine force
above.
Because there's nothing there, no guy with a big grey beard,
No ultimate warrior to fight our wars.
We make our own wars.
To think there is some kind of presence watching over us
Is, at the very least, misguided.

Existential Angst

There is a great deal more to our existence
Than what we have endured.
For this confrontation, we would never get insured,
Because it's a completely unknown reality
That no conventional mind could withstand,
In direct contradiction to life's banality—
Nothing to do with material wealth, or money in hand.

As money is nothing, have it or not,
We all go to a similar burial plot.
In a wooden box, we all will rot,
Unless it's cardboard, yes, spare a thought
For those who die and people cared not a jot.
How sad, dearly departed, that's your lot.

I believe our words and actions echo through time,
And in spite of this poem, they don't have to rhyme.
Make a contribution, however small,
And if you mean it, you can stand tall.
Because that means, despite it all,
With pride, you can face humanity's wall.
And feel no shame, only you are to blame.
Embrace and eviscerate everything negative in your name.

Before you move on, cleanse your soul.
Then, holding you back is nothing at all.

The Legacy of Self-Pity

They say, for things you've done wrong,
You gotta pay.
Well, that's not exactly right, I say.
We can truly repent in our own way.
If you carry the burden of guilt,
You pay the price.
For your transgressions every day,
Through the regret that holds you in a vice.

I would rather have taken my punishment
Than wallow in this cesspit of shame and despair,
And enjoy the comforting nourishment
Of being cleansed by honesty's clean and gentle air.

But I cannot, because I don't have a time machine.
It's just more filth added to life's latrine.
All the things I've done, all I've seen,
With but a few moments of redemption in between.

But they do not forgive my many terrible acts.
This is my story, and these are facts.
I have done nothing to deserve prison, in the conventional sense,
But I have served many years, looking at the four walls, hoping
to make amends.

I fear it will never happen, I will never be released
From this ugliest and most malevolent beast
That is my own mind, my self-made life sentence.
I have found hell, and wait by the entrance.

The West End

The best pint in town for the past sixty years,
Forget your problems, put aside your fears.
Sheila and Michael will give you their attention,
As best they can, without pretension.
A sober voice of reason, no judgement incurred,
Even after a few pints, when your words become slurred.
They've seen it all before, and think nothing of it,
Arguments, fights, even vomit.
Just so long as you show your respect,
And your manners you do not neglect.
I fear for the future, when the West End is no more,
And what's left are pubs I abhor.
Establishments that have no soul,
No faithful generations to enrol
Into the traditions which we hold so close,
The price of progress, I suppose.

The Haiku (HI-Q)

HI-Q? Probably Not.

Dirt, dust, and dead flies,
The detritus of neglect,
Keeps my mind busy.

I Didn't Used to Be Like This

At the tender age of 21, I lost my mind.
I had never felt such distress, such hell,
Inescapable in the extreme, my place I tried to find,
But my mind was gone, and my sense of self as well.
I no longer knew who I was, cast out to the abyss;
I had to find my own way back.
I didn't used to be like this.

I was arrogant, but responsible,
Before this happened, to be clear.
The arrogance has gone, but so has the responsibility, I fear.
I am a faint shadow of the man I could have been,
Something ghostly, a husk, with nothing to give;
No reason to care, no reason to live.
Not in life, nor in death, something in-between.

I see people from my youth, and I can tell,
When they look at me, I am, to them, a vision of hell.
And I don't know if they feel pity, but they always repel.
They want the conversation to be short, but I do as well.
For I feel just as uneasy as them, I'd rather give it a miss;
I didn't used to be like this.

My anxiety has taken over my everyday life,
I can't conduct myself like a normal person.
Much as I try, the infinite horrible possibilities
What I might do if I lose control dominates my mind.

The other day I was waiting in a queue,
I started to shake and sweat, and I saw people looking at me in disdain.
I tried to be normal, completely in vain.
The girl at the checkout glanced in disapproval,
No doubt signalling security for my removal.
She served me nonetheless, exchanging glances in all directions,
I struggled to compose myself, ignoring her fake vocal inflections.
When I exited the shop, I could hear her taking the piss,
At which point, against my better judgement, I turned around and said,
'Excuse me, Miss, but I didn't used to be like this.'

www.ingramcontent.com/pod-product-compliance
Lightning Source LLC
Chambersburg PA
CBHW051654060726
47593CB00021B/1265